SONNETS FROM THE PORTUGUESE
AND OTHER LOVE POEMS

ELIZABETH BARRETT BROWNING

SONNETS

FROM THE

PORTUGUESE

AND OTHER

LOVE POEMS

Illustrated by
ADOLF HALLMAN

HANOVER HOUSE, GARDEN CITY, NEW YORK

◆§ CONTENTS §◆

❧A NOTE ON
ELIZABETH BARRETT BROWNING❧

When Robert Browning met Elizabeth Barrett Moulton-Barrett for the first time, she had been for many years an invalid in her home at 50 Wimpole Street. The exact nature of her illness is uncertain. Mr. G. K. Chesterton says of her: "She was an invalid, and an invalid of a somewhat unique kind, and living beyond all question under very unique circumstances"; and he speaks later of "hysteria" and "neurosis." But whatever her illness may have been, it was real enough to her, and dangerously so at times. "The picture of helpless indolence" she calls herself; "sublimely helpless and impotent"; "I had done living I thought"; "Was ever life so like death before? My face was so close against the tombstones, that there seemed no room even for the tears." The thought comes often in the sonnets:

> Betwixt me and the dreadful outer brink
> Of obvious death, where I, who thought to sing . . .
>
> I yield the grave for thy sake, and exchange
> My near sweet view of Heaven, for earth with thee!
> Nor God's infliction, nor death's neighbourhood . . .

She speaks always of her life before the meeting with Browning as one of sadness. Yet her childhood, passed on her father's country estate, was a happy one, until at the age of fifteen the illness which was to haunt her life began. At this time, too, while saddling her pony, she injured herself in some way which was thought to have affected her spine, and this increased the delicacy of her health. She was a precocious child, who read Greek and wrote verses from very early days. A few years after the accident her mother died, and there remained to Elizabeth eight younger brothers, two sisters—and her father. Like the father of the Brontës, the father of the Barretts is one of the enigmas of literary history; he was a factor of overwhelming importance in that strange family. Chesterton says, "at last . . . she knew to all intents and purposes that she had grown up in the house of a madman."

To his children he was almost unbelievably despotic; and, especially, any suggestion of the possibility of marriage for any one of them seems to have driven him to fury. "Everyone you see . . . all my brothers . . . constrained bodily into submission . . . by that worst and most dishonouring of necessities, the necessity of living, every one of them all, except myself, being dependent in money matters on the inflexible will." But though she realized that her father was "a peculiar person," it is clear that for many years Elizabeth was genuinely devoted to him. Two crises in her life, before their final parting, affected her feelings toward him. The first was the death of her brother Edward—"my brother whom I loved so . . . the dearest

9

of friends and brothers in one . . . better than us all, and kindest and noblest and dearest to me, beyond comparison, any comparison . . ." After their mother died, the family had moved to Sidmouth, and then to London, where Elizabeth became very ill. "They sent me down you know to Torquay—Dr. Chambers saying that I could not live a winter in London. The worst—what people call the worst—was apprehended for me at that time. So I was sent down with my sister to my aunt there —and he, my brother whom I loved so, was sent too, to take us there and return." But when the time came for his return Elizabeth was so distressed that her father with great reluctance allowed him to remain, though he "considered it to be very *wrong in me to exact such a thing.*" Then, two years later, Edward was drowned at sea! It nearly killed Elizabeth. "For three days we waited—and I hoped while I could—oh—that awful agony of three days! . . . I, who could not speak or shed a tear, but lay for weeks and months half conscious, half unconscious, with a wandering mind . . . The spring of life . . . seemed to break within me *then.*" This tragedy in her life brought her father very near to her: "When . . . I lost what I loved best in the world beyond comparison and rivalship . . . I felt that he stood the nearest to me on the closed grave . . . he was generous and forbearing in that hour of bitter trial, and never reproached me as he might have done and as my own soul has not spared."

In the Dedication *"To My Father"* prefixed to the first edition of her *Poems* she says: "You, who have shared with me in things bitter and sweet, softening or enhancing them, every day . . . may accept from me the inscription of these volumes, the exponents of a few years of an existence which has been sustained and comforted by you as well as given . . . It is my fancy thus . . . to satisfy my heart while I sanctify my ambition, by associating with the great pursuit of my life its tenderest and holiest affection."

This is not the language of one oppressed beyond endurance, and at this time her father can hardly have been, to Elizabeth at least, the monster he has been represented; and it is worth remembering, perhaps, that this pathetic Dedication was reprinted in all editions of her *Poems* till her death—long after she had left him, never to be forgiven.

In 1841 she returned to Wimpole Street, to lead there for many years her invalid life, shut in her room, with "Flush, my dog" her chief companion and "loving friend."

> But of thee it shall be said,
> This dog watched beside a bed
>   Day and night unweary,
> Watched within a curtained room
> Where no sunbeam brake the gloom
>   Round the sick and dreary.

In the summer she would go out sometimes in a chair or carriage, or even, very rarely, for a walk. "I was out walking again to-day, and . . . I walked up all these stairs with my own feet on returning. I sat down on the stairs two or three times . . . and I was not carried, as usual—see how vainglorious I am." But in the winters she could hardly leave her room. "We all get used to the thought of a tomb, and I was buried, that was the whole." The second crisis in her relations with her father occurred after she and Browning had met, and must have made easier for her the decision to escape.

His character was "becoming gloomier and stranger as time went on."[1] In July 1845 he was "discussing the question" of sending Elizabeth abroad for the winter, yet in September, when her doctor urged the necessity of it, he deliberately made her going impossible. "Words have been said that I cannot easily forget, nor remember without pain . . . I told him that my prospects of health seemed to me to depend on taking this step . . . I feel aggrieved of course and wounded." Later she writes: "I had believed Papa to have loved me more than he obviously does"; and again: "If he had let me I should have loved him . . . Now it is too late . . ."

This weakening of her affection for her father must have influenced her later conduct profoundly, yet even before this time the greater influence of Browning had altered her whole outlook. They knew nothing of each other beyond their published works, but a common admiration served as introduction. "I love your verses with all my heart, dear Miss Barrett"—so begins one of the most fascinating correspondences in English literature.

This was in January 1845, and by May, after many letters and much hesitation on her part, Browning had overcome her "blind dislike of seeing strangers" and was admitted to see her for the first time. Two days later she received a letter—the only one in the long series to be destroyed—which must have amounted to a declaration of love. Her answer is preserved: "You do not know what pain you give me in speaking so wildly. You have said some intemperate things . . . fancies, —which you will forget at once, and for ever, having said at all . . . if there should be one word of answer attempted to this; or of reference; I must not . . . I will not see you again." But, on this condition, he might call on Tuesday.

He did call, and they continued to meet secretly once a week, until in September she wrote: "You have touched me more profoundly than I thought even you could have touched me . . . Henceforward I am yours for everything but to do you harm." For a full year more their meetings went on; both writing almost daily and sometimes twice a day; Browning urging her to marry him and fly to Italy, Elizabeth consenting but hesitant. "I will do what you please and as you please to have it done. But there is time for considering." During this time she must have been

[1] G. K. Chesterton, Robert Browning.

writing the Sonnets, but there is no mention of them in her letters. It was not lack of courage in either that made it impossible to face her father, but the absolute certainty of his refusal. "He would rather see me dead at his foot . . . We should be separated, you see, from *that moment*."

A secret elopement was the only possibility. "*Elopement*—— (But, dearest, nobody will use such a word surely to the event.)" At last the time came when they must decide at once or wait another year—Elizabeth's health would not allow a winter journey. They were married on Saturday, September 12, 1846, and she returned to Wimpole Street after the service: a week later, with Flush and her maid Wilson, they sailed for France. She never saw her father again; when, years later, they came back to England, the letters she had written him were sent to her unopened: Wimpole Street was closed against her. From Paris they went to Pisa, and there for the first time she showed the Sonnets to her husband. There is, of course, no Portuguese original for them. Browning admired especially her poem *Catarina to Camoens*, and had called her his "little Portuguese." It has been suggested that this may have been the origin of the purposely misleading title, which was not used until the Sonnets were published in 1850. Referring to their publication, Browning is reported to have said: "I dared not keep to myself the finest Sonnets written in any language since Shakespeare's."

SONNETS FROM THE PORTUGUESE

I thought once how Theocritus had sung
Of the sweet years, the dear and wished-for years,
Who each one in a gracious hand appears
To bear a gift for mortals, old or young:
And, as I mused it in his antique tongue,
I saw, in gradual vision through my tears,
The sweet, sad years, the melancholy years,
Those of my own life, who by turns had flung
A shadow across me. Straightway I was 'ware,
So weeping, how a mystic Shape did move
Behind me, and drew me backward by the hair;
And a voice said in mastery, while I strove,—
"Guess now who holds thee?"—"Death," I said. But, there,
The silver answer rang,—"Not Death, but Love."

But only three in all God's universe
Have heard this word thou hast said,—Himself, beside
Thee speaking, and me listening! and replied
One of us . . . *that* was God, . . . and laid the curse
So darkly on my eyelids, as to amerce
My sight from seeing thee,—that if I had died,
The deathweights, placed there, would have signified
Less absolute exclusion. "Nay" is worse
From God than from all others, O my friend!
Men could not part us with their worldly jars,
Nor the seas change us, nor the tempests bend;
Our hands would touch for all the mountain bars:
And, heaven being rolled between us at the end,
We should but vow the faster for the stars.

Unlike are we, unlike, O princely Heart!
Unlike our uses and our destinies.
Our ministering two angels look surprise
On one another, as they strike athwart
Their wings in passing. Thou, bethink thee, art
A quest for queens to social pageantries,
With gages from a hundred brighter eyes
Than tears even can make mine, to play thy part
Of chief musician. What hast thou to do
With looking from the lattice-lights at me,
A poor, tired, wandering singer, singing through
The dark, and leaning up a cypress tree?
The chrism is on thine head,—on mine, the dew,—
And Death must dig the level where these agree.

Thou hast thy calling to some palace-floor,
Most gracious singer of high poems! where
The dancers will break footing, from the care
Of watching up thy pregnant lips for more.
And dost thou lift this house's latch too poor
For hand of thine? and canst thou think and bear
To let thy music drop here unaware
In folds of golden fulness at my door?
Look up and see the casement broken in,
The bats and owlets builders in the roof!
My cricket chirps against thy mandolin.
Hush, call no echo up in further proof
Of desolation! there's a voice within
That weeps . . . as thou must sing . . . alone, aloof.

I lift my heavy heart up solemnly,
As once Electra her sepulchral urn,
And, looking in thine eyes, I overturn
The ashes at thy feet. Behold and see
What a great heap of grief lay hid in me,
And how the red wild sparkles dimly burn
Through the ashen greyness. If thy foot in scorn
Could tread them out to darkness utterly,
It might be well perhaps. But if instead
Thou wait beside me for the wind to blow
The grey dust up, . . . those laurels on thine head
O my Belovèd, will not shield thee so,
That none of all the fires shall scorch and shred
The hair beneath. Stand farther off then! go.

Go from me. Yet I feel that I shall stand
Henceforward in thy shadow. Nevermore
Alone upon the threshold of my door
Of individual life, I shall command
The uses of my soul, nor lift my hand
Serenely in the sunshine as before,
Without the sense of that which I forbore—
Thy touch upon the palm. The widest land
Doom takes to part us, leaves thy heart in mine
With pulses that beat double. What I do
And what I dream include thee, as the wine
Must taste of its own grapes. And when I sue
God for myself, He hears that name of thine,
And sees within my eyes the tears of two.

The face of all the world is changed, I think,
Since first I heard the footsteps of thy soul
Move still, oh, still, beside me, as they stole
Betwixt me and the dreadful outer brink
Of obvious death, where I, who thought to sink,
Was caught up into love, and taught the whole
Of life in a new rhythm. The cup of dole
God gave for baptism, I am fain to drink,
And praise its sweetness, Sweet, with thee anear.
The names of country, heaven, are changed away
For where thou art or shalt be, there or here;
And this . . . this lute and song . . . loved yesterday,
(The singing angels know) are only dear
Because thy name moves right in what they say.

What can I give thee back, O liberal
And princely giver, who hast brought the gold
And purple of thine heart, unstained, untold,
And laid them on the outside of the wall
For such as I to take or leave withal,
In unexpected largesse? am I cold,
Ungrateful, that for these most manifold
High gifts, I render nothing back at all?
Not so; not cold,—but very poor instead.
Ask God who knows. For frequent tears have run
The colours from my life, and left so dead
And pale a stuff, it were not fitly done
To give the same as pillow to thy head.
Go farther! let it serve to trample on.

Can it be right to give what I can give?
To let thee sit beneath the fall of tears
As salt as mine, and hear the sighing years
Re-sighing on my lips renunciative
Through those infrequent smiles which fail to live
For all thy adjurations? O my fears,
That this can scarce be right! We are not peers,
So to be lovers; and I own, and grieve,
That givers of such gifts as mine are, must
Be counted with the ungenerous. Out, alas!
I will not soil thy purple with my dust,
Nor breathe my poison on thy Venice-glass,
Nor give thee any love—which were unjust.
Beloved, I only love thee! let it pass.

Go from me. Yet I feel that I shall stand
Henceforward in thy shadow.

SONNET XIV

If thou must love me, let it be for nought
Except for love's sake only.

Yet, love, mere love, is beautiful indeed
And worthy of acceptation. Fire is bright,
Let temple burn, or flax; an equal light
Leaps in the flame from cedar-plank or weed:
And love is fire. And when I say at need
I love thee . . . mark! . . . I love thee—in thy sight
I stand transfigured, glorified aright,
With conscience of the new rays that proceed
Out of my face toward thine. There's nothing low
In love, when love the lowest: meanest creatures
Who love God, God accepts while loving so.
And what I *feel*, across the inferior features
Of what I *am*, doth flash itself, and show
How that great work of Love enhances Nature's.

And therefore if to love can be desert,
I am not all unworthy. Cheeks as pale
As these you see, and trembling knees that fail
To bear the burden of a heavy heart,—
This weary minstrel-life that once was girt
To climb Aornus, and can scarce avail
To pipe now 'gainst the valley nightingale
A melancholy music,—why advert
To these things? O Belovèd, it is plain
I am not of thy worth nor for thy place!
And yet, because I love thee, I obtain
From that same love this vindicating grace,
To live on still in love, and yet in vain,—
To bless thee, yet renounce thee to thy face.

Indeed this very love which is my boast,
And which, when rising up from breast to brow,
Doth crown me with a ruby large enow
To draw men's eyes and prove the inner cost,—
This love even, all my worth, to the uttermost,
I should not love withal, unless that thou
Hadst set me an example, shown me how,
When first thine earnest eyes with mine were crossed,
And love called love. And thus, I cannot speak
Of love even, as a good thing of my own:
Thy soul hath snatched up mine all faint and weak,
And placed it by thee on a golden throne,—
And that I love (O soul, we must be meek!)
Is by thee only, whom I love alone.

And wilt thou have me fasten into speech
The love I bear thee, finding words enough,
And hold the torch out, while the winds are rough,
Between our faces, to cast light on each?—
I drop it at thy feet. I cannot teach
My hand to hold my spirit so far off
From myself—me—that I should bring thee proof
In words, of love hid in me out of reach.
Nay, let the silence of my womanhood
Commend my woman-love to thy belief,—
Seeing that I stand unwon, however wooed,
And rend the garment of my life, in brief,
By a most dauntless, voiceless fortitude,
Lest one touch of this heart convey its grief.

If thou must love me, let it be for nought
Except for love's sake only. Do not say
"I love her for her smile—her look—her way
Of speaking gently,—for a trick of thought
That falls in well with mine, and certes brought
A sense of pleasant ease on such a day"—
For these things in themselves, Belovèd, may
Be changed, or change for thee,—and love, so wrought,
May be unwrought so. Neither love me for
Thine own dear pity's wiping my cheeks dry,—
A creature might forget to weep, who bore
Thy comfort long, and lose thy love thereby!
But love me for love's sake, that evermore
Thou mayst love on, through love's eternity.

Accuse me not, beseech thee, that I wear
Too calm and sad a face in front of thine;
For we two look two ways, and cannot shine
With the same sunlight on our brow and hair.
On me thou lookest with no doubting care,
As on a bee shut in a crystalline;
Since sorrow hath shut me safe in love's divine,
And to spread wing and fly in the outer air
Were most impossible failure, if I strove
To fail so. But I look on thee—on thee—
Beholding, besides love, the end of love,
Hearing oblivion beyond memory;
As one who sits and gazes from above,
Over the rivers to the bitter sea.

And yet, because thou overcomest so,
Because thou art more noble and like a king,
Thou canst prevail against my fears and fling
Thy purple round me, till my heart shall grow
Too close against thine heart henceforth to know
How it shook when alone. Why, conquering
May prove as lordly and complete a thing
In lifting upward, as in crushing low!
And as a vanquished soldier yields his sword
To one who lifts him from the bloody earth,
Even so, Belovèd, I at last record,
Here ends my strife. If *thou* invite me forth,
I rise above abasement at the word.
Make thy love larger to enlarge my worth.

My poet, thou canst touch on all the notes
God set between His After and Before,
And strike up and strike off the general roar
Of the rushing worlds a melody that floats
In a serene air purely. Antidotes
Of medicated music, answering for
Mankind's forlornest uses, thou canst pour
From thence into their ears. God's will devotes
Thine to such ends, and mine to wait on thine.
How, Dearest, wilt thou have me for most use?
A hope, to sing by gladly? or a fine
Sad memory, with thy songs to interfuse?
A shade, in which to sing—of palm or pine?
A grave, on which to rest from singing? Choose.

I never gave a lock of hair away
To a man, Dearest, except this to thee,
Which now upon my fingers thoughtfully,
I ring out to the full brown length and say
"Take it." My day of youth went yesterday;
My hair no longer bounds to my foot's glee,
Nor plant I it from rose or myrtle-tree,
As girls do, any more: it only may
Now shade on two pale cheeks the mark of tears,
Taught drooping from the head that hangs aside
Through sorrow's trick. I thought the funeral-shears
Would take this first, but Love is justified,—
Take it thou,—finding pure, from all those years,
The kiss my mother left here when she died.

The soul's Rialto hath its merchandise;
I barter curl for curl upon that mart,
And from my poet's forehead to my heart
Receive this lock which outweighs argosies,
As purply black, as erst to Pindar's eyes
The dim purpureal tresses gloomed athwart
The nine white Muse-brows. For this counterpart,
The bay-crown's shade, Belovèd, I surmise,
Still lingers on thy curl, it is so black!
Thus, with a fillet of smooth-kissing breath,
I tie the shadows safe from gliding back,
And lay the gift where nothing hindereth;
Here on my heart, as on thy brow, to lack
No natural heat till mine grows cold in death.

Belovèd, my Belovèd, when I think
That thou wast in the world a year ago,
What time I sat alone here in the snow
And saw no footprint, heard the silence sink
No moment at thy voice, but, link by link,
Went counting all my chains as if that so
They never could fall off at any blow
Struck by thy possible hand,—why, thus I drink
Of life's great cup of wonder! Wonderful,
Never to feel thee thrill the day or night
With personal act or speech,—nor ever cull
Some prescience of thee with the blossoms white
Thou sawest growing! Atheists are as dull,
Who cannot guess God's presence out of sight.

Say over again, and yet once over again,
That thou dost love me. Though the word repeated
Should seem "a cuckoo-song," as thou dost treat it,
Remember, never to the hill or plain,
Valley and wood, without her cuckoo-strain
Comes the fresh Spring in all her green completed.
Belovèd, I, amid the darkness greeted
By a doubtful spirit-voice, in that doubt's pain
Cry, "Speak once more—thou lovest!" Who can fear
Too many stars, though each in heaven shall roll,
Too many flowers, though each shall crown the year?
Say thou dost love me, love me, love me—toll
The silver iterance!—only minding, Dear,
To love me also in silence with thy soul.

When our two souls stand up erect and strong,
Face to face, silent, drawing nigh and nigher,
Until the lengthening wings break into fire
At either curvèd point,—what bitter wrong
Can the earth do to us, that we should not long
Be here contented? Think. In mounting higher,
The angels would press on us and aspire
To drop some golden orb of perfect song
Into our deep, dear silence. Let us stay
Rather on earth, Belovèd,—where the unfit
Contrarious moods of men recoil away
And isolate pure spirits, and permit
A place to stand and love in for a day,
With darkness and the death-hour rounding it.

Is it indeed so? If I lay here dead,
Wouldst thou miss any life in losing mine?
And would the sun for thee more coldly shine
Because of grave-damps falling round my head?
I marvelled, my Belovèd, when I read
Thy thought so in the letter. I am thine—
But . . . so much to thee? Can I pour thy wine
While my hands tremble? Then my soul, instead
Of dreams of death, resumes life's lower range.
Then, love me, Love! look on me—breathe on me!
As brighter ladies do not count it strange,
For love, to give up acres and degree,
I yield the grave for thy sake, and exchange
My near sweet view of Heaven, for earth with thee!

Let the world's sharpness, like a clasping knife,
Shut in upon itself and do no harm
In this close hand of Love, now soft and warm,
And let us hear no sound of human strife
After the click of the shutting. Life to life—
I lean upon thee, Dear, without alarm,
And feel as safe as guarded by a charm
Against the stab of worldlings, who if rife
Are weak to injure. Very whitely still
The lilies of our lives may reassure
Their blossoms from their roots, accessible
Alone to heavenly dews that drop not fewer,
Growing straight, out of man's reach, on the hill.
God only, who made us rich, can make us poor.

A heavy heart, Belovèd, have I borne
From year to year until I saw thy face,
And sorrow after sorrow took the place
Of all those natural joys as lightly worn
As the stringèd pearls, each lifted in its turn
By a beating heart at dance-time. Hopes apace
Were changed to long despairs, till God's own grace
Could scarcely lift above the world forlorn
My heavy heart. Then *thou* didst bid me bring
And let it drop adown thy calmly great
Deep being! Fast it sinketh, as a thing
Which its own nature doth precipitate,
While thine doth close above it, mediating
Betwixt the stars and the unaccomplished fate.

I lived with visions for my company
Instead of men and women, years ago,
And found them gentle mates, nor thought to know
A sweeter music than they played to me.
But soon their trailing purple was not free
Of this world's dust, their lutes did silent grow,
And I myself grew faint and blind below
Their vanishing eyes. Then *thou* didst come—to be,
Belovèd, what they seemed. Their shining fronts,
Their songs, their splendours (better, yet the same,
As river-water hallowed into fonts),
Met in thee, and from out thee overcame
My soul with satisfaction of all wants:
Because God's gifts put man's best dreams to shame.

My own Belovèd, who hast lifted me
From this drear flat of earth where I was thrown,
And, in betwixt the languid ringlets, blown
A life-breath, till the forehead hopefully
Shines out again, as all the angels see,
Before thy saving kiss! My own, my own,
Who camest to me when the world was gone,
And I who looked for only God, found thee!
I find thee; I am safe, and strong, and glad.
As one who stands in dewless asphodel
Looks backward on the tedious time he had
In the upper life,—so I, with bosom-swell,
Make witness, here, between the good and bad,
That Love, as strong as Death, retrieves as well.

My letters! all dead paper, mute and white!
And yet they seem alive and quivering
Against my tremulous hands which loose the string
And let them drop down on my knee to-night.
This said,—he wished to have me in his sight
Once, as a friend: this fixed a day in spring
To come and touch my hand . . . a simple thing,
Yet I wept for it!—this, . . . the paper's light . . .
Said, *Dear, I love thee;* and I sank and quailed
As if God's future thundered on my past.
This said, *I am thine*—and so its ink has paled
With lying at my heart that beat too fast.
And this . . . O Love, thy words have ill availed
If, what this said, I dared repeat at last!

I think of thee!—my thoughts do twine and bud
About thee, as wild vines, about a tree,
Put out broad leaves, and soon there's nought to see
Except the straggling green which hides the wood.
Yet, O my palm-tree, be it understood
I will not have my thoughts instead of thee
Who art dearer, better! Rather, instantly
Renew thy presence; as a strong tree should,
Rustle thy boughs and set thy trunk all bare,
And let these bands of greenery which insphere thee
Drop heavily down,—burst, shattered, everywhere!
Because, in this deep joy to see and hear thee
And breathe within thy shadow a new air,
I do not think of thee—I am too near thee.

I see thine image through my tears to-night
And yet to-day I saw thee smiling. How
Refer the cause?—Belovèd, is it thou
Or I, who makes me sad? The acolyte
Amid the chanted joy and thankful rite
May so fall flat, with pale insensate brow,
On the altar-stair. I hear thy voice and vow,
Perplexed, uncertain, since thou art out of sight,
As he, in his swooning ears, the choir's Amen.
Belovèd, dost thou love? or did I see all
The glory as I dreamed, and fainted when
Too vehement light dilated my ideal,
For my soul's eyes? Will that light come again,
As now these tears come—falling hot and real?

Thou comest! all is said without a word.
I sit beneath thy looks, as children do
In the noon-sun, with souls that tremble through
Their happy eyelids from an unaverred
Yet prodigal inward joy. Behold, I erred
In that last doubt! and yet I cannot rue
The sin most, but the occasion—that we two
Should for a moment stand unministered
By a mutual presence. Ah, keep near and close,
Thou dovelike help! and, when my fears would rise,
With thy broad heart serenely interpose:
Brood down with thy divine sufficiencies
These thoughts which tremble when bereft of those,
Like callow birds left desert to the skies.

SONNET XX

Belovèd, my Belovèd, when I think
That thou wast in the world a year ago,
What time I sat alone here in the snow
And saw no footprint, heard the silence sink . . .

My own Belovèd, who hast lifted me
From this dear flat of earth where I was thrown,
And, in betwixt the languid ringlets, blown
A life-breath, till the forehead hopefully
Shines out again, as all the angels see,
Before thy saving kiss!

The first time that the sun rose on thine oath
To love me, I looked forward to the moon
To slacken all those bonds which seemed too soon
And quickly tied to make a lasting troth.
Quick-loving hearts, I thought, may quickly loathe;
And, looking on myself, I seemed not one
For such man's love!—more like an out-of-tune
Worn viol, a good singer would be wroth
To spoil his song with, and which, snatched in haste,
Is laid down at the first ill-sounding note.
I did not wrong myself so, but I placed
A wrong on *thee*. For perfect strains may float
'Neath master-hands, from instruments defaced,—
And great souls, at one stroke, may do and doat.

Yes, call me by my pet-name! let me hear
The name I used to run at, when a child,
From innocent play, and leave the cowslips piled,
To glance up in some face that proved me dear
With the look of its eyes. I miss the clear
Fond voices which, being drawn and reconciled
Into the music of Heaven's undefiled,
Call me no longer. Silence on the bier,
While I call God—call God!—So let thy mouth
Be heir to those who are now exanimate.
Gather the north flowers to complete the south,
And catch the early love up in the late.
Yes, call me by that name,—and I, in truth,
With the same heart, will answer and not wait.

With the same heart, I said, I'll answer thee
As those, when thou shalt call me by my name—
Lo, the vain promise! is the same, the same,
Perplexed and ruffled by life's strategy?
When called before, I told how hastily
I dropped my flowers or brake off from a game,
To run and answer with the smile that came
At play last moment, and went on with me
Through my obedience. When I answer now,
I drop a grave thought, break from solitude;
Yet still my heart goes to thee—ponder how—
Not as to a single good, but all my good!
Lay thy hand on it, best one, and allow
That no child's foot could run fast as this blood.

If I leave all for thee, wilt thou exchange
And be all to me? Shall I never miss
Home-talk and blessing and the common kiss
That comes to each in turn, nor count it strange,
When I look up, to drop on a new range
Of walls and floors, another home than this?
Nay, wilt thou fill that place by me which is
Filled by dead eyes too tender to know change?
That's hardest. If to conquer love, has tried,
To conquer grief, tries more, as all things prove;
For grief indeed is love and grief beside.
Alas, I have grieved so I am hard to love.
Yet love me—wilt thou? Open thine heart wide,
And fold within the wet wings of thy dove.

When we met first and loved, I did not build
Upon the event with marble. Could it mean
To last, a love set pendulous between
Sorrow and sorrow? Nay, I rather thrilled,
Distrusting every light that seemed to gild
The onward path, and feared to overlean
A finger even. And, though I have grown serene
And strong since then, I think that God has willed
A still renewable fear . . . O love, O troth . . .
Lest these enclaspèd hands should never hold,
This mutual kiss drop down between us both
As an unowned thing, once the lips being cold.
And Love, be false! if *he*, to keep one oath,
Must lose one joy, by his life's star foretold.

Pardon, oh, pardon, that my soul should make,
Of all that strong divineness which I know
For thine and thee, an image only so
Formed of the sand, and fit to shift and break.
It is that distant years which did not take
Thy sovranty, recoiling with a blow,
Have forced my swimming brain to undergo
Their doubt and dread, and blindly to forsake
Thy purity of likeness and distort
Thy worthiest love to a worthless counterfeit:
As if a shipwrecked Pagan, safe in port,
His guardian sea-god to commemorate,
Should set a sculptured porpoise, gills a-snort
And vibrant tail, within the temple-gate.

First time he kissed me, he but only kissed
The fingers of this hand wherewith I write;
And ever since, it grew more clean and white,
Slow to world-greetings, quick with its "Oh, list,"
When the angels speak. A ring of amethyst
I could not wear here, plainer to my sight,
Than that first kiss. The second passed in height
The first, and sought the forehead, and half missed,
Half falling on the hair. O beyond meed!
That was the chrism of love, which love's own crown,
With sanctifying sweetness, did precede.
The third upon my lips was folded down
In perfect, purple state; since when, indeed,
I have been proud and said, "My love, my own."

Because thou hast the power and own'st the grace
To look through and behind this mask of me
(Against which years have beat thus blanchingly
With their rains), and behold my soul's true face,
The dim and weary witness of life's race,—
Because thou hast the faith and love to see,
Through that same soul's distracting lethargy,
The patient angel waiting for a place
In the new Heavens,—because nor sin nor woe,
Nor God's infliction, nor death's neighbourhood,
Nor all which others viewing, turn to go,
Nor all which makes me tired of all, self-viewed,—
Nothing repels thee, . . . Dearest, teach me so
To pour out gratitude, as thou dost, good!

Oh, yes! they love through all this world of ours!
I will not gainsay love, called love forsooth.
I have heard love talked in my early youth,
And since, not so long back but that the flowers
Then gathered, smell still. Mussulmans and Giaours
Throw kerchiefs at a smile, and have no ruth
For any weeping. Polypheme's white tooth
Slips on the nut if, after frequent showers,
The shell is over-smooth,—and not so much
Will turn the thing called love, aside to hate
Or else to oblivion. But thou art not such
A lover, my Belovèd! thou canst wait
Through sorrow and sickness, to bring souls to touch,
And think it soon when others cry "Too late."

I thank all who have loved me in their hearts,
With thanks and love from mine. Deep thanks to all
Who paused a little near the prison-wall
To hear my music in its louder parts
Ere they went onward, each one to the mart's
Or temple's occupation, beyond call.
But thou, who, in my voice's sink and fall
When the sob took it, thy divinest Art's
Own instrument didst drop down at thy foot
To hearken what I said between my tears, . . .
Instruct me how to thank thee! Oh, to shoot
My soul's full meaning into future years,
That *they* should lend it utterance, and salute
Love that endures, from Life that disappears!

"My future will not copy fair my past"—
I wrote that once; and thinking at my side
My ministering life-angel justified
The word by his appealing look upcast
To the white throne of God, I turned at last,
And there, instead, saw thee, not unallied
To angels in thy soul! Then I, long tried
By natural ills, received the comfort fast,
While budding, at thy sight, my pilgrim's staff
Gave out green leaves with morning dews impearled.
I seek no copy now of life's first half:
Leave here the pages with long musing curled,
And write me new my future's epigraph,
New angel mine, unhoped for in the world!

How do I love thee? Let me count the ways.
I love thee to the depth and breadth and height
My soul can reach, when feeling out of sight
For the ends of Being and ideal Grace.
I love thee to the level of everyday's
Most quiet need, by sun and candle-light.
I love thee freely, as men strive for Right;
I love thee purely, as they turn from Praise.
I love thee with the passion put to use
In my old griefs, and with my childhood's faith.
I love thee with a love I seemed to lose
With my lost saints,—I love thee with the breath,
Smiles, tears, of all my life!—and, if God choose,
I shall but love thee better after death.

Belovèd, thou hast brought me many flowers
Plucked in the garden, all the summer through
And winter, and it seemed as if they grew
In this close room, nor missed the sun and showers.
So, in the like name of that love of ours,
Take back these thoughts which here unfolded too,
And which on warm and cold days I withdrew
From my heart's ground. Indeed, those beds and bowers
Be overgrown with bitter weeds and rue,
And wait thy weeding; yet here's eglantine,
Here's ivy!—take them, as I used to do
Thy flowers, and keep them where they shall not pine.
Instruct thine eyes to keep their colours true,
And tell thy soul their roots are left in mine.

❧OTHER LOVE POEMS❧

We cannot live, except thus mutually
We alternate, aware or unaware,
The reflex act of life: and when we bear
Our virtue onward most impulsively,
Most full of invocation, and to be
Most instantly compellant, certes, there
We live most life, whoever breathes most air
And counts his dying years by sun and sea.
But when a soul, by choice and conscience, doth
Throw out her full force on another soul,
The conscience and the concentration both
Make mere life, Love. For Life in perfect whole
And aim consummated, is Love in sooth,
As nature's magnet-heat rounds pole with pole.

I

She has laughed as softly as if she sighed,
    She has counted six and over,
Of a purse well filled, and a heart well tried—
    Oh each a worthy lover!
They "give her time;" for her soul must slip
    Where the world has set the grooving:
She will lie to none with her fair red lip—
    But love seeks truer loving.

II

She trembles her fan in a sweetness dumb,
    As her thoughts were beyond recalling,
With a glance for one, and a glance for some,
    For her eyelids rising and falling;
Speaks common words with a blushful air,
    Hears bold words, unreproving;
But her silence says—what she never will swear—
    And love seeks better loving.

III

Go, lady, lean to the night-guitar,
    And drop a smile to the bringer,
Then smile as sweetly, when he is far,
    At the voice of an indoor singer.
Bask tenderly beneath tender eyes;
    Glance lightly on their removing;
And join new vows to old perjuries—
    But dare not call it loving.

IV

Unless you can think, when the song is done,
　　No other is soft in the rhythm;
Unless you can feel, when left by one,
　　That all men else go with him;
Unless you can know, when unpraised by his breath,
　　That your beauty itself wants proving;
Unless you can swear, "For life, for death!"—
　　Oh fear to call it loving!

V

Unless you can muse in a crowd all day,
　　On the absent face that fixed you;
Unless you can love, as the angels may,
　　With the breadth of heaven betwixt you;
Unless you can dream that his faith is fast,
　　Through behoving and unbehoving;
Unless you can die when the dream is past—
　　Oh never call it loving!

I

Love me, sweet, with all thou art,
    Feeling, thinking, seeing,—
Love me in the lightest part,
    Love me in full being.

II

Love me with thine open youth
    In its frank surrender;
With the vowing of thy mouth,
    With its silence tender.

III

Love me with thine azure eyes,
    Made for earnest granting!
Taking color from the skies,
    Can Heaven's truth be wanting?

IV

Love me with their lids, that fall
    Snow-like at first meeting:
Love me with thine heart, that all
    The neighbors then see beating.

V

Love me with thine hand stretched out
    Freely—open-minded:
Love me with thy loitering foot,—
    Hearing one behind it.

VI

Love me with thy voice, that turns
   Sudden faint above me;
Love me with thy blush that burns
   When I murmur "Love me!"

VII

Love me with thy thinking soul—
   Break it to love-sighing;
Love me with thy thoughts that roll
   On through living—dying.

VIII

Love me with thy gorgeous airs,
   When the world has crowned thee!
Love me, kneeling at thy prayers,
   With the angels round thee.

IX

Love me pure, as musers do,
   Up the woodlands shady:
Love me gaily, fast, and true,
   As a winsome lady.

X

Through all hopes that keep us brave,
   Further off or nigher,
Love me for the house and grave,—
   And for something higher.

Thus, if thou wilt prove me, dear,
Woman's love no fable,
I will love *thee*—half-a-year—
As a man is able.

I

Five months ago the stream did flow,
  The lilies bloomed within the sedge,
And we were lingering to and fro
Where none will track thee in this snow,
  Along the stream, beside the hedge.
Ah, sweet, be free to love and go!
  For, if I do not hear thy foot,
  The frozen river is as mute,
  The flowers have dried down to the root:
  And why, since these be changed since May,
    Shouldst thou change less than they?

II

And slow, slow as the winter snow,
  The tears have drifted to mine eyes;
And my poor cheeks, five months ago
Set blushing at thy praises so,
  Put paleness on for a disguise.
Ah, sweet, be free to praise and go!
  For, if my face is turned too pale,
  It was thine oath that first did fail;
  It was thy love proved false and frail:
  And why, since these be changed enow,
    Should I change less than thou?

SONNET XXXV

If I leave all for thee, wilt thou exchange
And be all to me?

SONNET XLI
    I thank all who have loved me in their hearts,
    With thanks and love from mine.

I

Sweet, thou hast trod on a heart.
　　Pass; there's a world full of men;
And women as fair as thou art
　　Must do such things now and then.

II

Thou only hast stepped unaware;
　　Malice, not one can impute;
And why should a heart have been there,
　　In the way of a fair woman's foot?

III

It was not a stone that could trip,
　　Nor was it a thorn that could rend:
Put up thy proud underlip!
　　'Twas merely the heart of a friend.

IV

And yet, peradventure, one day
　　Thou, sitting alone at the glass,
Remarking the bloom gone away,
　　Where the smile in its dimplement was,

V

And seeking around thee in vain,
　　From hundreds who flattered before,
Such a word as, "Oh, not in the main
　　Do I hold thee less precious, but more!" . . .

VI

Thou'lt sigh, very like, on thy part,
  "Of all I have known or can know,
I wish I had only that heart
  I trod upon ages ago!"

God be with thee my beloved,—God be with thee!
  Else alone thou goest forth,
  Thy face unto the north,
Moor and pleasance all around thee and beneath thee
  Looking equal in one snow!
  While I try to reach thee,
  Vainly follow, vainly follow,
  With the farewell and the hollo,
  And cannot reach thee so.
  Alas! I can but teach thee.
God be with thee my beloved,—God be with thee!

Can I teach thee, my beloved—can I teach thee?
  If I said, Go left or right,
  The counsel would be light,
The wisdom, poor of all that could enrich thee!
  My right would show like left;
  My raising would depress thee,
  My choice of light would blind thee,
  Of way, would leave behind thee,
  Of end, would leave bereft!
  Alas! I can but bless thee—
May God teach thee my beloved,—may God teach thee!

Can I bless thee, my beloved,—can I bless thee?
  What blessing word can I,
  From mine own tears, keep dry?
What flowers grow in my field wherewith to dress thee?
  My good reverts to ill;
  My calmnesses would move thee,
  My softnesses would prick thee,
  My bindings up would break thee,
  My crownings, curse and kill.
  Alas! I can but love thee.
May God bless thee my beloved,—may God bless thee!

Can I love thee, my beloved,—can I love thee?
    And is *this* like love, to stand
    With no help in my hand,
When strong as death I fain would watch above thee?
    My love-kiss can deny
    No tears that fall beneath it:
    Mine oath of love can swear thee
    From no ill that comes near thee,—
    And thou diest while I breathe it,
    And I—*I* can but die!
May God love thee my beloved,—may God love thee!

I

I stand by the river where both of us stood,
And there is but one shadow to darken the flood;
And the path leading to it, where both used to pass,
Has the step of but one to take dew from the grass,—
    One forlorn since that day.

II

The flowers of the margin are many to see;
None stoops at my bidding to pluck them for me.
The bird in the alder sings loudly and long:
My low sound of weeping disturbs not his song,
    As thy vow did that day.

III

I stand by the river, I think of the vow;
Oh, calm as the place is, vow-breaker, be thou!
I leave the flower growing, the bird unreproved:
Would I trouble *thee* rather than *them*, my beloved,—
    And my lover that day?

IV

Go, be sure of my love, by that treason forgiven;
Of my prayers, by the blessings they win thee from heaven;
Of my grief (guess the length of the sword by the sheath's)
By the silence of life, more pathetic than death's!
    Go,—be clear of that day!

Mine eyes are weary of surveying
The fairest things, too soon decaying;
Mine ears are weary of receiving
The kindest words—ah, past believing!
Weary my hope, of ebb and flow;
Weary my pulse, of tunes of woe:
My trusting heart is weariest!
I would—I would, I were at rest!

For me, can earth refuse to fade?
For me, can words be faithful made?
Will my embitter'd hope be sweet?
My pulse forego the human beat?
No! Darkness must consume mine eye
Silence, mine ear—hope cease—pulse die
And o'er mine heart a stone be press'd—
Or vain this,—"Would I were at rest!"

There is a land of rest deferr'd:
Nor eye hath seen, nor ear hath heard,
Nor Hope hath trod the precinct o'er;
For Hope beheld its hope no more!
There, human pulse forgets its tone
There, hearts may know as they are known!
Oh, for dove's wings, thou dwelling blest,
To fly to thee, and be at rest!

I

You love all, you say,
   Round, beneath, above me:
Find me then some way
   Better than to love me,
Me, too, dearest May!

II

O world-kissing eyes
   Which the blue heavens melt to!
I, sad, overwise,
   Loathe the sweet looks dealt to
All things—men and flies.

III

You love all, you say:
   Therefore, Dear, abate me—
Just your love, I pray!
   Shut your eyes and hate me
Only me—fair May!

I

I classed, appraising once,
Earth's lamentable sounds,—the welladay,
    The jarring yea and nay,
The fall of kisses on unanswering clay,
The sobbed farewell, the welcome mournfuller;
    But all did leaven the air
With a less bitter leaven of sure despair
    Than these words, "I loved once."

II

And who saith "I loved once"?
Not angels, whose clear eyes, love, love, foresee,
    Love, through eternity,
And by *To Love* to apprehend *To Be.*
Not God, called *Love*, his noble crown-name casting
    A light too broad for blasting:
The great God changing not from everlasting,
    Saith never, "I loved once."

III

Oh, never is "Loved once"
Thy word, thou Victim-Christ, misprizèd friend!
    Thy cross and curse may rend,
But, having loved, thou lovest to the end.
This is man's saying,—man's: too weak to move
    One spherèd star above,
Man desecrates the eternal God-word Love
    By his No More and Once.

75

IV

How say ye, "We loved once,"
Blasphemers? Is your earth not cold enow,
 Mourners, without that snow?
Ah, friends, and would ye wrong each other so?
And could ye say of some whose love is known,
 Whose prayers have met your own,
Whose tears have fallen for you, whose smiles have shown
 So long, "We loved them once"?

V

Could ye, "We loved her once,"
Say calm of me, sweet friends, when out of sight?
 When hearts of better right
Stand in between me and your happy light?
Or when, as flowers kept too long in the shade,
 Ye find my colors fade,
And all that is not love in me decayed?
 Such words,—ye loved me once!

VI

Could ye, "We loved her once,"
Say cold of me when further put away
 In earth's sepulchral clay,
When mute the lips which deprecate today?
Not so! not then—least then! When life is shriven,
 And death's full joy is given,
Of those who sit and love you up in heaven,
 Say not "We loved them once."

VII

Say never, ye loved once:
God is too near above, the grave, beneath,
   And all our moments breathe
Too quick in mysteries of life and death
For such a word. The eternities avenge
   Affections light of range.
There comes no change to justify that change,
   Whatever comes,—Loved once!

And yet that same word once
Is humanly acceptive. Kings have said,
   Shaking a discrowned head,
"We ruled once,"—dotards, "We once taught and led;"
Cripples once danced i' the vines; and bards approved
   Were once by scornings moved:
But love strikes one hour—love! those never loved
   Who dream that they loved once.

I

"Yes," I answered you last night;
   "No," this morning, sir, I say:
Colors seen by candle-light
   Will not look the same by day.

II

When the viols played their best,
   Lamps above, and laughs below,
Love me sounded like a jest,
   Fit for yes, or fit for *no*.

III

Call me false, or call me free,
   Vow, whatever light may shine,
No man on your face shall see
   Any grief for change on mine.

IV

Yet the sin is on us both;
   Time to dance is not to woo:
Wooing light makes fickle troth,
   Scorn of me recoils on you.

V

Learn to win a lady's faith
   Nobly, as the thing is high,
Bravely, as for life and death.
   With a loyal gravity.

VI

Lead her from the festive boards,
    Point her to the starry skies;
Guard her by your truthful words
    Pure from courtship's flatteries.

VII

By your truth she shall be true,
    Ever true, as wives of yore;
And her "Yes" once said to you
    Shall be Yes for evermore.

I

We walked beside the sea
After a day which perished silently
Of its own glory—like the Princess weird
Who, combating the Genius, scorched and seared,
Uttered with burning breath, "Ho! victory!"
And sank adown an heap of ashes pale.
    So runs the Arab tale.

II

The sky above us showed
An universal and unmoving cloud,
On which the cliffs permitted us to see
Only the outline of their majesty,
As master minds, when gazed at by the crowd!
And, shining with a gloom, the water grey
    Swang in its moon-taught way.

III

Nor moon, nor stars were out.
They did not dare to tread so soon about,
Though trembling, in the footsteps of the sun.
The light was neither night's nor day's, but one
Which, life-like, had a beauty in its doubt:
And Silence's impassioned breathings round
    Seemed wandering into sound.

IV

O solemn-beating heart
Of nature! I have knowledge that thou art
Bound unto man's by cords he cannot sever—
And, what time they are slackened by him ever,
So to attest his own supernal part,
Still runneth thy vibration fast and strong,
  The slackened cord along.

V

For though we never spoke
Of the grey water and the shaded rock,
Dark wave and stone unconsciously were fused
Into the plaintive speaking that we used
Of absent friends and memories unforsook;
And, had we seen each other's face, we had
  Seen haply, each was sad.

Fair Amy of the terraced house,
   Assist me to discover
Why you who would not hurt a mouse
   Can torture so your lover.

You give your coffee to the cat,
   You stroke the dog for coming,
And all your face grows kinder at
   The little brown bee's humming.

But when *he* haunts your door . . . the town
   Marks coming and marks going . . .
You seem to have stitched your eyelids down
   To that long piece of sewing!

You never give a look, not you,
   Nor drop him a "Good morning,"
To keep his long day warm and blue,
   So fretted by your scorning.

She shook her head—"The mouse and bee
   For crumb or flower will linger:
The dog is happy at my knee,
   The cat purrs at my finger.

"But *he* . . . to *him*, the least thing given
   Means great things at a distance;
He wants my world, my sun, my heaven,
   Soul, body, whole existence.

"They say love gives as well as takes;
    But I'm a simple maiden,—
My mother's first smile when she wakes
    I still have smiled and prayed in.

"I only know my mother's love
    Which gives all and asks nothing;
And this new loving sets the groove
    Too much the way of loathing.

"Unless he gives me all in change,
    I forfeit all things by him:
The risk is terrible and strange—
    I tremble, doubt, . . . deny him.

"He's sweetest friend or hardest foe,
    Best angel or worst devil;
I either hate or . . . love him so,
    I can't be merely civil!

"You trust a woman who puts forth
    Her blossoms thick as summer's?
You think she dreams what love is worth,
    Who casts it to new-comers?

"Such love's a cowslip-ball to fling,
    A moment's pretty pastime;
I give . . . all me, if anything,
    The first time and the last time.

"Dear neighbor of the trellised house,
   A man should murmur never,
Though treated worse than dog and mouse,
   Till doated on for ever!"

I

Fast this Life of mine was dying,
  Blind already and calm as death,
Snowflakes on her bosom lying
  Scarcely heaving with her breath.

II

Love came by, and having known her
  In a dream of fabled lands,
Gently stooped, and laid upon her
  Mystic chrism of holy hands;

III

Drew his smile across her folded
  Eyelids, as the swallow dips;
Breathed as finely as the cold did
  Through the locking of her lips.

IV

So, when Life looked upward, being
  Warmed and breathed on from above,
What sight could she have for seeing,
  Evermore . . . but only Love?

I

We have met late—it is too late to meet,
    O friend, not more than friend!
Death's forecome shroud is tangled round my feet,
And if I step or stir, I touch the end.
    In this last jeopardy
Can I approach thee, I, who cannot move?
How shall I answer thy request for love?
    Look in my face and see.

II

I love thee not, I dare not love thee! Go
    In silence; drop my hand.
If thou seek roses, seek them where they blow
In garden-alleys, not in desert-sand.
    Can life and death agree,
That thou shouldst stoop thy song to my complaint?
I cannot love thee. If the word is faint,
    Look in my face and see.

III

I might have loved thee in some former days.
    Oh, then, my spirits had leapt
As now they sink, at hearing thy love-praise!
Before these faded cheeks were overwept,
    Had this been asked of me,
To love thee with my whole strong heart and head,
I should have said still . . . yes, but *smiled* and said,
    "Look in my face and see!"

86

IV

But now . . . God sees me, God, who took my heart
   And drowned it in life's surge.
In all your wide warm earth I have no part—
A light song overcomes me like a dirge.
   Could Love's great harmony
The saints keep step to when their bonds are loose,
Not weigh me down? am I a wife to choose?
   Look in my face and see—

V

While I behold, as plain as one who dreams,
   Some woman of full worth,
Whose voice, as cadenced as a silver stream's,
Shall prove the fountain-soul which sends it forth;
   One younger, more thought-free
And fair and gay, than I, thou must forget,
With brighter eyes than these . . . which are not wet . . .
   Look in my face and see!

VI

So farewell thou, whom I have known too late
   To let thee come so near.
Be counted happy while men call thee great,
And one belovèd woman feels thee dear!—
   Not I!—that cannot be.
I am lost, I am changed,—I must go farther, where
The change shall take me worse, and no one dare
   Look in my face and see.

VII

Meantime I bless thee. By these thoughts of mine
   I bless thee from all such!
I bless thy lamp to oil, thy cup to wine,
Thy hearth to joy, thy hand to an equal touch
   Of loyal troth. For me,
I love thee not, I love thee not!—away!
Here's no more courage in my soul to say
   "Look in my face and see."

Love you seek for, presupposes
　　Summer heat and sunny glow,
Tell me, do you find moss-roses
　　Budding, blooming in the snow?
Snow might kill the rose-tree's root—
Shake it quickly from your foot,
　　Lest it harm you as you go.

From the ivy where it dapples
　　A grey ruin, stone by stone,
Do you look for grapes or apples,
　　Or for sad green leaves alone?
Pluck the leaves off, two or three—
Keep them for morality
　　When you shall be safe and gone.

THE LADY'S "YES"

"Yes," I answered you last night;
"No," this morning, sir, I say:
Colors seen by candle-light
Will not look the same by day.

PROOF AND DISPROOF
Dost thou love me, my Belovèd?
Who shall answer yes or no?

I

I love thee, love thee, Giulio;
  Some call me cold, and some demure;
And if thou hast ever guessed that so
  I loved thee . . . well, the proof was poor
    And no one could be sure.

II

Before thy song (with shifted rhymes
  To suit my name) did I undo
The persian? If it stirred sometimes,
  Thou hast not seen a hand push through
    A foolish flower or two.

III

My mother listening to my sleep,
  Heard nothing but a sigh at night,—
The short sigh rippling on the deep,
  When hearts run out of breath and sight
    Of men, to God's clear light.

IV

When others named thee,—thought thy brows
  Were straight, thy smile was tender—"Here
He comes between the vineyard-rows!"
  I said not "Ay," nor waited, Dear,
    To feel thee step too near.

V

I left such things to bolder girls,—
   Olivia or Clotilda. Nay,
When that Clotilda, through her curls,
   Held both thine eyes in hers one day,
     I marvelled, let me say.

VI

I could not try the woman's trick:
   Between us straightway fell the blush
Which kept me separate, blind and sick.
   A wind came with thee in a flush,
     As blown through Sinai's bush.

VII

But now that Italy invokes
   Her young men to go forth and chase
The foe or perish,—nothing chokes
   My voice, or drives me from the place.
     I look thee in the face.

VIII

I love thee! It is understood,
   Confest: I do not shrink or start.
No blushes! all my body's blood
   Has gone to greaten this poor heart.
     That, loving, we may part.

IX

Our Italy invokes the youth
    To die if need be. Still there's room,
Though earth is strained with dead in truth:
    Since twice the lilies were in bloom
        They have not grudged a tomb.

X

And many a plighted maid and wife
    And mother, who can say since then
"My country,"—cannot say through life
    "My son," "my spouse," "my flower of men,"
        And not weep dumb again.

XI

Heroic males the country bears,—
    But daughters give up more than sons:
Flags wave, drums beat, and unawares
    You flash your souls out with the guns,
        And take your Heaven at once.

XII

But we!—we empty heart and home
    Of life's life, love! We bear to think
You're gone,—to feel you may not come,—
    To hear the door-latch stir and clink,
        Yet no more you! . . . nor sink.

XIII

Dear God! when Italy is one,
  Complete, content from bound to bound,
Suppose, for my share, earth's undone
  By one grave in 't—as one small wound
    Will kill a man, 't is found.

XIV

What then? If love's delight must end,
  At least we'll clear its truth from flaws.
I love thee, love thee, sweetest friend!
  Now take my sweetest without pause,
    And help the nation's cause.

XV

And thus, of noble Italy
  We'll both be worthy! Let her show
The future how we made her free,
  Nor sparing life . . . nor Giulio,
    Nor this . . . this heartbreak! Go.

I

Dost thou love me, my Belovèd?
  Who shall answer yes or no?
What is provèd or disprovèd
  When my soul inquireth so,
Dost thou love me, my Belovèd?

II

I have seen thy heart to-day,
  Never open to the crowd,
While to love me aye and aye
  Was the vow as it was vowed
By thine eyes of steadfast grey.

III

Now I sit alone, alone—
  And the hot tears break and burn,
Now, Belovèd, thou art gone,
  Doubt and terror have their turn.
Is it love that I have known?

IV

I have known some bitter things,—
  Anguish, anger, solitude.
Year by year an evil brings,
  Year by year denies a good;
March winds violate my springs.

V

I have known how sickness bends,
    I have known how sorrow breaks,—
How quick hopes have sudden ends,
    How the heart thinks till it aches
Of the smile of buried friends.

VI

Last, I have known *thee*, my brave
    Noble thinker, lover, doer!
The best knowledge last I have.
    But thou comest as the thrower
Of fresh flowers upon a grave.

VII

Count what feelings used to move me!
    Can this love assort with those?
Thou, who art so far above me,
    Wilt thou stoop so, for repose?
Is it true that thou canst love me?

VIII

Do not blame me if I doubt thee.
    I can call love by its name
When thine arm is wrapt about me;
    But even love seems not the same,
When I sit alone, without thee.

IX

In thy clear eyes I descried
　　Many a proof of love, to-day;
But to-night, those unbelied
　　Speechful eyes being gone away,
There's the proof to seek, beside.

X

Dost thou love me, my Belovèd?
　　Only *thou* canst answer yes!
And, thou gone, the proof's disprovèd,
　　And the cry rings answerless—
Dost thou love me, my Belovèd?

I

There is no one beside thee, and no one above thee;
   Thou standest alone, as the nightingale sings!
   Yet my words that would praise thee are impotent things,
For none can express thee though all should approve thee!
I love thee so, Dear, that I only can love thee.

II

Say, what can I do for thee? . . . weary thee . . . grieve thee?
   Lean on my shoulder . . . new burdens to add?
   Weep my tears over thee . . . making thee sad?
Oh, hold me not—love me not? let me retrieve thee!
I love thee so, Dear, that I only can leave thee.

I

Oh, wilt thou have my hand, Dear, to lie along in thine?
As a little stone in a running stream, it seems to lie and pine!
Now drop the poor pale hand, Dear, . . . unfit to plight with thine.

II

Oh, wilt thou have my cheek, Dear, drawn closer to thine own?
My cheek is white, my cheek is worn, by many a tear run down.
Now leave a little space, Dear, . . lest it should wet thine own.

III

Oh, must thou have my soul, Dear, commingled with thy soul?—
Red grows the cheek, and warm the hand, . . . the part is in the whole! . . .
Nor hands nor cheeks keep separate, when soul is joined to soul.

CATARINA TO CAMOENS

*(Dying in his absence abroad, and referring to the poem
in which he recorded the sweetness of her eyes)*

On the door you will not enter,
   I have gazed too long—adieu!
Hope withdraws her peradventure—
   Death is near me,—and not you!
     Come, O lover!
     Close and cover
These poor eyes, you called, I ween,
"Sweetest eyes, were ever seen."

When I heard you sing that burden
   In my vernal days and bowers,
Other praises disregarding,
   I but hearkened that of yours,—
     Only saying
     In heart-playing,
"Blessed eyes mine eyes have been,
If the sweetest, *his* have seen!"

But all changes. At this vesper,
   Cold the sun shines down the door.
If you stood there, would you whisper
   "Love, I love you," as before,—
     Death pervading
     Now, and shading
Eyes you sang of, that yestreen,
As the sweetest ever seen?

Yes! I think, were you beside them,
  Near the bed I die upon,—
Though their beauty you denied them,
  As you stood there looking down,
    You would truly
    Call them duly,
For the love's sake found therein,—
"Sweetest eyes, were ever seen."

And if you looked down upon them,
  And if *they* looked up to you,
All the light which has foregone them
  Would be gathered back anew!
    They would truly
    Be as duly
Love-transformed to Beauty's sheen,—
"Sweetest eyes, were ever seen."

But, ah me! you only see me
  In your thoughts of loving man,
Smiling soft perhaps and dreamy
  Through the wavings of my fan,—
    And unweeting
    Go repeating,
In your reverie serene,
"Sweetest eyes, were ever seen."

While my spirit leans and reaches
    From my body still and pale,
Fain to hear what tender speech is
    In your love to help my bale—
        O my poet
        Come and show it!
Come, of latest love to glean
"Sweetest eyes, were ever seen."

O my poet, O my prophet,
    When you praised their sweetness so,
Did you think, in singing of it,
    That it might be near to go?
        Had you fancies
        From their glances,
That the grave would quickly screen
"Sweetest eyes, were ever seen?"

No reply! The fountains warble
    In the court-yard sounds alone:
As the water to the marble
    So my heart falls with a moan,
        From love-sighing
        To this dying!
Death forerunneth Love, to win
"Sweetest eyes, were ever seen."

Will you come? when I'm departed
   Where all sweetnesses are hid—
When thy voice, my tender-hearted,
   Will not lift up either lid,
     Cry, O lover,
     Love is over!
Cry beneath the cypress green—
"Sweetest eyes, were ever seen."

When the angelus is ringing,
   Near the convent will you walk,
And recall the choral singing
   Which brought angels down our talk?
     Spirit-shriven
     I viewed Heaven,
Till you smiled—"Is earth unclean,
Sweetest eyes, were ever seen?"

When beneath the palace-lattice,
   You ride slow as you have done,
And you see a face there—*that* is
   Not the old familiar one,—
     Will you oftly
     Murmur softly,
"Here, ye watched me morn and e'en,
Sweetest eyes, were ever seen!"

When the palace ladies sitting
   Round your gittern, shall have said,
"Poet, sing those verses written
   For the lady who is dead,"
     Will you tremble,
     Yet dissemble,—
Or sing hoarse, with tears between,
"Sweetest eyes, were ever seen?"

Sweetest eyes! How sweet in flowings,
   The repeated cadence is!
Though you sang a hundred poems,
   Still the best one would be this.
     I can hear it
     'Twixt my spirit
And the earth noise intervene—
"Sweetest eyes, were ever seen."

But the priest waits for the praying,
   And the choir are on their knees,
And the soul must pass away in
   Strains more solemn high than these!
     Miserere
     For the weary—
Oh, no longer for Catrine,
"Sweetest eyes, were ever seen!"

Keep my riband, take and keep it,
    I have loosed it from my hair;
Feeling, while you overweep it,
    Not alone in your despair,
        Since with saintly
        Watch, unfaintly,
Out of Heaven shall o'er you lean
"Sweetest eyes, were ever seen."

But—but *now*—yet unremoved
    Up to Heaven, they glisten fast:
You may cast away, Belovèd,
    In your future all my past;
        Such old phrases
        May be praises
For some fairer bosom-queen—
"Sweetest eyes, were ever seen!"

Eyes of mine, what are ye doing?
    Faithless, faithless—praised amiss
If a tear be of your showing,
    Drop for any hope of *his*!
        Death hath boldness
        Besides coldness,
If unworthy tears demean
"Sweetest eyes, were ever seen."

I will look out to his future—
   I will bless it till it shine:
Should he ever be a suitor
   Unto sweeter eyes than mine,
     Sunshine gild them,
     Angels shield them,
Whatsoever eyes terrene
Be the sweetest *his* have seen!

Oh rose! who dares to name thee?
No longer roseate now, nor soft, nor sweet;
But pale, and hard, and dry, as stubble wheat,—
    Kept seven years in a drawer—thy titles shame thee.

The breeze that used to blow thee
Between the hedge-row thorns, and take away
An odor up the lane to last all day,—
    If breathing now,—unsweetened would forego thee.

The sun that used to smite thee,
And mix his glory in thy gorgeous urn,
Till beam appeared to bloom, and flower to burn,—
    If shining now,—with not a hue would light thee.

The dew that used to wet thee,
And, white first, grow incarnadined, because
It lay upon thee where the crimson was,—
    If dropping now, would darken where it met thee.

The fly that lit upon thee,
To stretch the tendrils of his tiny feet,
Along thy leaf's pure edges, after heat,—
    If lighting now, would coldly overrun thee.

The bee that once did suck thee,
And build thy perfumed ambers up his hive,
And swoon in thee for joy, till scarce alive,—
    If passing now, would blindly overlook thee.

The heart doth recognize thee,
Alone, alone! The heart doth smell thee sweet,
Doth view thee fair, doth judge thee most complete—
    Though seeing now those changes that disguise thee.

    Yes, and the heart doth owe thee
More love, dead rose! than to such roses bold
As Julia wears at dances, smiling cold!—
    Lie still upon this heart—which breaks below thee!